I. Introduction

Entry and exit by firms are driving forces of economic growth and key elements of the competitive process. For example, recent research finds that virtually all of the labor productivity growth in the retail sector in the late 1990s was the result of entry and expansion of high productivity firms and the exit of less productive firms (Foster et al. 2006). Antitrust authorities too have long recognized that entry into markets can play an important role in maintaining competition. The U.S. government's primary policy document describing merger policy, the 2010 Department of Justice/Federal Trade Commission Horizontal Merger Guidelines, states that, "a merger is not likely to enhance market power if entry is so easy that the merged firm and its remaining rivals in the market, either unilaterally or collectively, could not profitably raise price or otherwise reduce competition."[2] However, determining whether entry would be easy and sufficient to replace the loss of competition resulting from a merger has proven to be difficult. Werden and Froeb (1988), for example, examine models with Cournot and Bertrand competition and find that with plausible levels of sunk costs that anticompetitive mergers are unlikely to generate entry. Further, for those cases where entry would occur following a merger, mergers would not be profitable *unless* they generated sufficient efficiencies such that the merger would not be anticompetitive to begin with. Notwithstanding this finding, courts have found that evidence of likelihood of entry into a market substantially lessens the concern that a merger in that market would be harmful (see, e.g., U.S. v. Syufy Enterprise (1990) and U.S. v. Baker Hughes (1990).

Surprisingly, given the importance of entry in antitrust analysis, there is relatively little detailed economic research examining market dynamics in the narrowly product categories which are often the focus of antitrust analysis.[3] To help fill this gap, our paper measures market dynamics during a recent six-year period (2004-2009) among three types of food retailers, traditional supermarkets, supercenters, and club stores that we

---

[2] U.S. Department of Justice and Federal Trade Commission Horizontal Merger Guidelines (2010), Section 9.

[3] Notable exceptions are studies of the cement (e.g., Syverson (2008), airline (e.g., Goolsbee and Syverson (2008), and banking industries (e.g., Berger et al. (2004).

refer to as the "big-box grocery retailing industry." This industry is a particularly interesting and important industry in which to study entry. Retail markets are often viewed as markets in which entry and expansion should be relatively easy, and the threat of entry is often seen to be sufficient to maintain competition (U.S. v. Syufy Enterprise (1990)). Indeed, relative to some sectors, the requirements to enter a retail market are not particularly onerous. Retailers need to identify an effective location and obtain permission from local regulators to open an establishment. The sunk costs of entry (e.g., the cost of structures and permits), in particular, are likely much lower than in most industries. Notwithstanding the perceived ease of entry and expansion, mergers in retail markets are often subject to material antitrust review. Between 1998 and 2007, for example, the FTC investigated supermarket mergers affecting 153 antitrust markets and challenged mergers in 134 of those markets.[4] Evidence on observed market dynamics in a retail market provides important information which can allow regulators to predict how likely potential entry or expansion by incumbents can be in lessening the competitive impact of mergers.

Our paper has four major findings. First, we examine changes in the composition of retail outlets in operation. While we find that the number of big-box grocery outlets operating in the U.S. has remained roughly constant at 31,000, each year roughly 7% of retail outlets either open or close. During our sample period, retailers operating club stores and supercenters have rapidly expanded at the expense of traditional supermarkets. However, even though the share of sales taking place at traditional supermarkets has declined, these retailers continue to open new stores each year representing roughly 2% of the stock of existing stores. We also find that while the average size of stores has increased over time, this change is largely the result of the expansion of retail formats using very large store sizes (club stores and supercenters) rather than an increase in the size of stores within formats.

Second, we examine entry by retail brands (defined as the operating name of the retail outlet such as Safeway or Albertsons) into new markets. We find that entry and exit are quite common for small independent supermarkets— single outlet firms—and

---

[4] Horizontal Merger Investigation Data, Fiscal Years 1996-2007, Federal Trade Commission, Table 4-2. Available at http://www.ftc.gov/os/2008/12/081201hsrmergerdata.pdf.

supermarkets owned by small chains (with less than 100 stores). Brand entry by chains operating large supermarket chains, however, is much more rare, and exit by large supermarket chains is three times as likely as entry (reflecting, in large part, the relative decline of traditional supermarkets). Entry by clubs and supercenters into non-rural markets is rare, however, this is largely a result of the fact that the firms operating these formats are already participants in most larger U.S. markets at the beginning of our sample period. In contrast to traditional supermarket retailers, we observe virtually no exit by firms operating clubs stores and supercenter retailers. We also find that other than in the smallest geographic markets, entrants rarely gain substantial (larger than 5%) revenue shares in the two years following entry. Thus, while entry is common for small firms, it is rare to observe entrants obtain a substantial share of industry revenue shortly after market entry.

Third, we find that within market expansion and contraction by incumbent retail brands is responsible for more, often much more, of the change in the number of stores operated by retail brands than either entry or exit. Supermarket chains added 963 stores as the result of entry into new markets during our sample period while chains expanded operations in markets in which they already participated by 1,882 stores. Analogous to our findings with entry, during our sample we see club and supercenter retailers significantly expand their operations in existing markets and virtually never observe these retailers contract their operations.

Finally, we examine the change in the relative size of market participants within a market over our sample period. We measure this "market churn" by taking the minimum of the aggregate net loss in establishments operated by shrinking brands and the aggregate net gain of brands that were expanding. We interpret this measure of turnover as the gain of growing brands that took place at the expense of shrinking brands. We find that most medium, large, and metro big-box grocery markets experience significant churn. For example, half of all metro markets experience banner churn of at least 11% between 2004 and 2009, that is, in these markets shrinking brands (collectively) shrink their operations by at least 11% (by closing stores) while expanding firms (collectively) expand their operations by at least 11%.

Our paper adds to a recent and growing literature analyzing market dynamics in retail markets. These papers fall into two broad categories. Literature in the first category examines a broad set of retailers over time rather than focusing on a narrow class of retailers serving a single industry market. Foster et al. (2006) estimate productivity growth in the U.S. retail sector using data from three rounds of the U.S. Census of Retail Trade (CRT) (1987, 1992, 1997) and find that most productivity growth is the result of the expansion and/or entry of large efficient firms coupled with the contraction and/or exit of smaller inefficient firms. Haltiwanger et al. (2010) uses a very detailed dataset describing the location and employment of all retailers within the Washington D.C. metro area to examine how the entry of Big-Box retailers affects nearby competing retailers. They find that the effects of Big-Box competition are localized: small chains and independent retailers are most negatively affected if the entering Big-Box store is located close by and operates in the same detailed industry. Basker et al. (2010) study general merchandise retailers using seven waves of the CRT (1977-2007) and find that surviving retailers have grown substantially over time both by expanding the number of stores they operate and the types of products they sell. Finally, Kosova and LaFontaine (2010) examine the importance of firm size and age in predicting the survival and growth of a broad set of franchised retail chains.

The second category focuses on competition among a narrow set of competitors like that analyzed in our paper. Many of these papers examine how WalMart's rapid expansion as a mass-merchandiser and more recently as a grocery retailer affects labor markets (Basker (2005a) and Ciccarella et al. (2008)) and consumer prices (Basker (2005b), Basker and Noel (2009), and Hausman and Liebtag (2007)). Matsa (2009) finds that competing supermarkets lower their service levels (measured by likelihood of a stockout) in response to entry of a WalMart supercenter. Ellickson and Grieco (2011) estimate the impact of Walmart's supercenter entry on the performance of nearby supermarkets. They find that rivals located nearby are negatively affected, mostly through an increase in the rate of decline of already weak firms. In contrast to the studies of WalMart supercenter entry, Courtemanche and Carden (2011) find that supermarkets do not lower their prices in response to club store entry. Instead, they find that entry by Costco supercenters is associated with an increase in supermarket prices while entry by

Sam's Club has essentially no impact on supermarket prices. Their finding is consistent with consumers that continue shopping at supermarkets having less elastic demand than those that shop at club stores.

More generally, Ellickson (2007) and Igami (2011) study the supermarket industry in the U.S. and Japan. Using a cross-section of data from 1998 Ellickson measures market structure in local markets throughout the U.S. and concludes that the U.S. supermarket industry is best modeled as natural oligopoly. Igami (2011) examines how entry and exit decisions by incumbent supermarkets changed in response to a major change in Japanese retail deregulation which facilitated entry by large supermarkets in the greater Tokyo region. He finds that an entry by a large supermarket increases the likelihood of exit for large and medium incumbent supermarkets while it increases the survival rate for small supermarkets.

Finally, our paper contributes to the extensive literature on market entry.[5] Klepper and Thompson (2006) develop a model which predicts that in mature markets, entry will take place in new segments (or submarkets) rather than in an existing technology. They provide empirical support for their model from the laser industry. Our finding that most entry and a large fraction of expansion in big-box grocery retailing, a very mature industry, is driven by retailers offering relatively new differentiated products (club stores and supercenters) aligns with Klepper and Thompson's predictions.

The remainder of the paper is organized as follows. Section II describes the retailers we are studying, and the construction of the markets they compete in. Section III describes our data source and Section IV presents our results. Section V concludes.

II. Institutional Background

We limit our attention to large grocery retailers that sell food and other household goods, e.g. cleaning products, where consumers can purchase all of their food for a week at a single retail location (often referred to as offering one-stop-shopping). This definition yields a market we refer to as "big-box" grocery retailers consisting of three

---

[5] See Geroski (1995) for a detailed literature review and Baker (2003) for a discussion of the recent treatment of entry in Horizontal Merger analysis.

different retail formats: traditional supermarkets, club stores, and supercenters. Our market excludes a number of retail formats that carry but do not specialize in selling food and other household goods, and firms that specialize in food but do not offer one-stop-shopping. Drug stores, convenience stores, and traditional mass merchandisers (non-supercenter outlets of firms such as Target, Kmart, and WalMart), for example, only offer a limited selection of food items and offer few of the perishable items which most consumers purchase weekly such as fresh meat and produce. These different retail formats are likely distant substitutes to big-box food retailers, and their exclusion is therefore unlikely to mask important industry dynamics.[6]

A traditional supermarket is defined as a self-service retailer selling a full line of food products (including grocery, meat, and produce).[7] There is substantial variation across geographic markets in establishment size, services offered, and the number of retail outlets operated by a supermarket firm. Not surprisingly, population density and the price of land are important in determining the size of supermarkets. In old, densely populated urban areas supermarkets are small, often with less than 20 thousand square feet of grocery selling space, while in newly developed suburban areas, supermarkets can be enormous (with grocery space and total selling space of 80 and 100 thousand square feet, respectively). As supermarkets expand in size they often increase the products and services available in the store including pharmacies, in-store bakeries, full-service delis, extensive wine and beer selections, bank branches, and even dry cleaners.

Following the recent literature which examines dynamics by firm size, e.g., Foster et al. (2006), we have divided our supermarket sample into three groups based on firm size: independents (1 store), small chains (between 2 and 100 stores), and large chains

---

[6] Previous empirical work discussed above shows that supermarkets change their prices in response to competition from supercenters and club retailers suggesting that these retail formats compete with one another. We are unaware of empirical work that directly measures substitution between big box grocery retailers and other types of food retailers. We do note that in its investigations of supermarket mergers the Federal Trade Commission (FTC) has typically concluded that competition among supermarkets is primarily limited to other supermarkets. For example, in its complaint challenging the merger of A&P and Pathmark in 2007, the FTC stated "Retail stores other than supermarkets that sell food and grocery products including neighborhood "mom & pop" grocery stores, convenience stores, specialty food stores, club stores, military commissaries, and mass merchants do not individually or collectively effectively constrain prices at supermarkets." See" Complaint in the Matter of The Great Atlantic and Pacific Tea Company INC., a corporation and Pathmark Stores Inc., a corporation" available at http://www.ftc.gov/os/caselist/0710120/0710120cmplt.pdf.
[7] See the Food Marketing Institute's Supermarket Facts available at: http://www.fmi.org/facts_figs/?fuseaction=superfact.

(with more than 100 stores). [8] While these groups are somewhat arbitrary, the sample is divided fairly evenly with 29% of stores operated by independents, 25% of supermarkets owned by small chains, and the remaining 46% of supermarkets owned by large chains.

Supercenters are an important and rapidly growing big-box grocery retail format. Supercenters are typically larger than 180,000 square feet, combining both a large supermarket and a large mass-merchandiser within the same store. The most well-known supercenter retailer, Wal-Mart, opened its first supercenter in 1988 and is now the U.S.'s largest food retailer.[9]

The third big-box grocery retail format is the club store. Club stores are high volume retailers that typically charge members an annual fee and offer a limited selection of a broad variety of products, including food items, usually in relatively large packages at significant volume discounts. A key difference between club stores and traditional supermarkets or supercenters is product selection; supermarkets or supercenters typically carry between 45,000 and 140,000 items while a club store may stock less than 4,000 at any point in time.[10] Despite their limited product offerings, club stores sell food in a large number of food categories, including meat and produce, and likely offer consumers the opportunity to purchase all of their food items at a single outlet; that is, a club store offers something very close to one-stop-shopping. According to Costco's 2009 Annual Report, 33% of Costco's sales were of food items with 12% of total Costco sales being Fresh Food items (including meat, bakery, deli, and produce). Given the very large sales volume of club stores (the average Costco outlet has $131 million in annual revenue), a typical club store sells more food items in a week than a very large traditional supermarket.

Table 1 provides some descriptive information about the establishments operating in the big-box grocery retail industry by format. The first 7 columns of Table 1 provide information on the distribution of estimated weekly grocery sales (in thousands of dollars) while the next seven columns describe the amount of selling space devoted to grocery items for the different firms operating in big-box grocery retail. Clearly,

---

[8] We define firm size as the total number of supermarket, club, and supercenter outlets operated by the firm.
[9] Supermarket news list available at: http://supermarketnews.com/sndata/.
[10] Costco 2009 Annual Report, page 9.

traditional supermarkets are much smaller retailers than either supercenters or club stores. The largest supermarkets (the 90th percentile of the large chain distribution is roughly $475 thousand per week) have similar estimated weekly sales than the smallest club stores and supercenters (the 10th percentile is $625 and $425 thousand per week, respectively). Supermarkets in large chains are both larger and have greater revenue, on average, than supermarkets in small chains, although there is considerable overlap in the two distributions. In contrast, independents are much smaller and have much lower revenue than either large or small supermarket chain outlets. Finally, supermarkets in large chains appear somewhat more homogeneous than those in small chains: both the standard deviation of store size and estimated weekly establishment sales are smaller for large chains than small chains despite a significantly larger mean.

Market Types

In order to define market entry and exit we must first define the geographic regions in which firms in the big-box grocery retail industry operate.[11] Unfortunately, market definition is not obvious and very different approaches have been taken in the literature. Many studies which focus on localized competition between retailers use relatively small geographic market definitions such as a county. This definition is reasonable when using a demand-side definition of a market: consumers do not travel far to purchase food and are likely most familiar with the retailers in operation near where they live and work. Empirical work suggests that localized competition is relevant in affecting supermarket pricing (See *e.g.*, Basker and Noel (2009)). A very narrow geographic market definition, however, ignores commercial connections with surrounding counties that affect firm store opening and closing decisions. Therefore a more expansive definition of geographic markets may be appropriate for explaining a firm's decision to incrementally expand the size of its chain. For example, a supermarket chain that is present only in Los Angeles County, California will be more likely to open a

---

[11] We are not attempting to construct antitrust markets (product and geographic) like those described in the *Horizontal Merger Guidelines*. Instead, as we describe in great detail below, we are focusing on identifying the set of similar retailers providing similar retail services (big-box-grocery retailing) and the geographic regions in which the firms either currently operate stores or could readily expand. In most cases, antitrust markets are likely smaller than the markets we consider here.

new establishment in Ventura County, California than in Fairfax County, Virginia.[12] Consumers in Ventura County will likely be familiar with the brand name of the Los Angeles based chain, a distribution network is already present, and experienced employees may be transferred to the new store without the various costs of relocation. Ellickson (2007), for example, defines the geographic regions in which retailers compete by focusing on the supply side: the distribution area used by supermarkets (corresponding to the region that stores can be served by a single distribution center). Ellickson argues that this definition is appropriate because firms can expand their operations within these broad regions with relatively little additional fixed or sunk costs and so it better reflects the level at which the firm is operated. Using this definition, Ellickson divides the U.S. into 51 geographic markets.

Our goal is to define markets that divide the U.S. into a series of mutually exclusive and completely exhaustive regions where each region is composed of political regions (counties) that share important commercial connections. By defining markets using commercial connections we incorporate the demand and supply concepts used in previous work in defining local retail markets. This is the approach taken by the Office of Management and Budget (OMB) in its construction of regional markets. We use two OMB geographic designations to construct these markets – Core Based Statistical Area (CBSA) and Combined Statistical Area (CSA). A CBSA is defined as a set of adjacent counties connected to a common urban core of at least 10,000 residents by commuting ties. A CSA is a consolidation of contiguous CBSAs that have a weaker but still significant employment interchange.[13] The rule we used in constructing geographic markets was to create the largest connected region. That is, if a store is in a county that belongs to a CBSA, the market for that store was defined to be at least as big as that CBSA, while if a store is located in a CBSA that belongs to a CSA, then that store's market is the CSA.

The result is a set of geographic markets that are mutually exclusive, cover the entire United States, and that represent regions that are economically connected to each

---

[12] As empirical support for this intuitive claim, we later show that large chain retailers are much more likely to open stores within a metro region they currently operate in than in a new metro region.
[13] The official standards for defining these areas are available at the OMB website. See: http://www.whitehouse.gov/sites/default/files/omb/fedreg/metroareas122700.pdf

other.[14] These geographic markets may consist of a single county or as many as 33 counties. The typical number of counties in a market is small, the median being 1 and the 95th percentile being 4. The median population for a market consisting of a single county is 10,627. The market with the largest population in our data, New York-Northern New Jersey-Long Island, NY-NJ-PA, consists of 30 counties.

In presenting our results we have grouped these geographic markets into four categories based on estimated population: Rural/Small City, Medium City, Large City, and Metro. Rural/Small City market corresponds to any market with a population under 100,000; Medium City corresponds to a unit for which the population is at least 100,000 but less than 1,000,000; Large City corresponds to a unit for which the population is at least 1,000,000, but less than 5,000,000; while Metro corresponds to a unit for which the population at least 5,000,000. While these break points do not evenly divide the U.S. population, they divide regions of the U.S. into meaningful groups with similar levels of population density.

Table 2 presents the number of markets of each type we study and describes the mean number of stores and revenue share for each retailer type for each of the four types of geographic markets we study.[15] We categorized 1,593 markets as Rural/Small City that collectively account for 12.7% of the U.S. population. The mean Rural/Small City market has 1.2 independent supermarkets, 1.04 small chain supermarkets, and 0.88 supermarkets owned by a large chain. While Club stores are very rare in Rural/Small City markets (0.02), these markets have 0.42 supercenters on average. Not surprisingly, the number of stores in markets increases dramatically as the market size grows. It is worth noting that the type of ownership of supermarkets also appears to be related to market size. In Rural/Small City and Medium City markets, independent and small chain supermarkets are relatively common while in Large City and Metro markets supermarkets owned by large chains make up a much larger fraction of total establishments within a geographic market.

---

[14] While all of the counties were included in the classification process, only geographic units for which at least one store was in operation at the beginning of the period were included in the analysis.

[15] The mean number of stores in a market type is calculated by counting the number of stores in each market and year by store type. These counts are then averaged by market type. The mean market share is calculated in a similar manner by summing the revenue of all stores in a particular store type for each market and year and then averaging by market type. Markets with 0 stores of a particular store type in a given year were counted as having 0 stores and having 0% share in that year.

III. Data

Our primary dataset comes from A.C. Nielsen's Trade Dimensions retail database. Each year, the firm creates a census of all retail outlets in the U.S. for a number of retailing industries including, for example, supermarkets, club stores, liquor stores, convenience stores, and restaurants. We have obtained data for conventional supermarkets, supercenters, and club stores.[16] Our dataset consists of annual observations including the location, size, estimated sales, a unique store number, the owner of the store, and estimated number of employees of each supermarket, supercenter, and club store in the U.S. from 2004 through the fall of 2009. A nice feature of the dataset is that every store location has a unique identification number that allows us to track stores over time. For example, we can observe if a location changes ownership or whether a supermarket that closes for a time and reopens as another supermarket. Additionally, the dataset contains information on the ownership of different chains which is important because many firms operate multiple retail brands, sometimes even within a relatively small geographic area.

We have also obtained annual county-level information from the Census including population estimates that allow us to construct and categorize the geographic markets in which the firms compete.

IV. Results

In this section we present the paper's empirical findings. First, we show that while the number of retail outlets operated in the big-box grocery industry has remained relatively constant in our sample period, there is significant turnover in the physical outlets operating within the industry each year. Some of this turnover is the result of a major change taking place within food retailing: the relative decline of traditional supermarkets and growth of club and supercenter retailers. Despite this ongoing trend, we observe a large number of both store closings and openings of supermarkets. We next

---

[16] We exclude other retail formats in the Trade Dimensions Grocery data set – limited assortment, natural/gourmet food, warehouse, and military commissary – because they are so differentiated from traditional supermarkets. For example, of these retail formats, only military commissaries offer one-stop-shopping. However, military commissaries are available to only a subset of the population.

develop some stylized facts describing within market dynamics. We find that market entry and exit by independent supermarkets and supermarkets operated by small chains is relatively common but that entry by large chain retailers is considerably rarer. Further, other than in relatively small markets, entrants rarely gain significant revenue shares within two years of market entry. We also find that market expansion and contraction by incumbent brands is responsible for more within market growth (contraction) than either entry or exit. Finally, we measure the change in relative market share- within market gains by expanding firms and contraction by shrinking firms, and find evidence that the relative position of retail brands changes significantly in many markets during our sample period.

Changes in the Composition of Retail Outlets

We begin by presenting a simple count of the number of retail outlets operated each year for each of the five retailer types (Table 3). In Table 3, we see that the number of retail outlets in the industry has been relatively constant, at roughly 31,000, between 2004 and 2009. This aggregate stability masks a significant change in the composition of retail outlets being operated over time. During our sample period the number of outlets operated as supermarkets declined by roughly 5% while the number of supercenters and club outlets expanded by 53.1% and 16.4%, respectively. Similarly, as shown in Figure 1, we see the revenue received by supermarkets has declined substantially, from 66.6% to 57.6%, while revenue shares for supercenters and clubs increased over the period – from 21.1% to 29.4% and from 12.3% to 13.0%, respectively.

While some of the changes in the composition of retail outlets operated in the U.S. are caused by the relative expansion of club and supercenter retailers, we also observe considerable turnover among the stores operated as traditional supermarkets. To show this we measure the number of store openings and closings for each retailer type. We define a store opening in year t as a new store location appearing in our dataset for the first time in period t. A store closing in year t is defined as a store that was present in year t-1 disappearing from the dataset in year t.[17] Figure 2 shows the overall rate of

---

[17] In a small number of cases a store disappears from the data for one or more periods and later reappears with the same store name. This event is likely either the result of a long-term store remodeling or, possibly,

openings and closings for the years 2005 through 2008 relative to the total number of stores operated within each retail format.[18] We see that across retailer types, turnover is substantial. Conventional supermarket retailers both opened and closed between 2-3% of their stores each year, with store closings being more common than openings during the sample period. In contrast, supercenter and club store retailers frequently open new stores (supercenters increased their stock of stores by more than 10% in 2005 and 2006) and almost never close existing stores.

Having established that retailers frequently open and close stores, we now examine how three characteristics of stores (size, revenue, and labor productivity) differ among newly opened, closed, and continuously operated retail outlets. Table 4 presents the mean size of the retail outlet store devoted to selling grocery items (thousands of square feet of grocery selling space), the estimated weekly sales of grocery items, and an outlet's estimated total weekly sales per employee separately for independent supermarket, chain supermarkets, supercenters, and club stores.[19] We find that for most store categories, store performance (measured as grocery revenue or total revenue per employee) is greatest for continuing stores and smallest for exiting stores. Stores that operate continuously are larger on average than either those that are being opened or closed throughout the sample period. For chain supermarkets and club stores, newly opened stores are of very similar size as closing stores, suggesting that store locations or possibly firms are being replaced rather than changes in the breadth of product offerings within a store. In contrast, the average opening supercenter outlet is 12.5% larger than a closing supercenter outlet. Finally, newly opened supermarkets operated by independents are 14.0% smaller on average than closing stores.

---

measurement error in the dataset and is not categorized as either a store opening or closing. Store locations that change ownership, e.g., assets that change ownership as the result of a merger or acquisition, are not categorized as either store openings or closings.

[18] To be more precise, the graph shows the number of opened stores in the year (openings) and the number of stores that are in operation, but will not be in operation in the next year (closings) divided by the number of stores of a particular format in operation in that year (total number of stores).

[19] Trade Dimensions reports an estimated number of employees for the outlet; that is, both employees selling grocery items and non-grocery items. For this reason, we calculate worker productivity as the ratio of total sales (both grocery and non-grocery items) per employee. For traditional supermarkets grocery sales make up the majority of sales, however, for club and supercenter outlets grocery sales are less than ½ of total sales. Club stores do not have reliable employee counts, and so are excluded from this calculation.

The results in Table 4 describe how new, closed, and continuously operated stores compare throughout the U.S. without controlling for market type (rural or metro markets) or firm. Store size and revenue, however, vary significantly across both retail firms and markets. To examine how opening, closing, and continuously operated stores compare holding these factors fixed, we have estimated equations (1)-(3) below separately for chain supermarkets, club stores, and supercenters where in each equation i denotes the store, j the chain, and k the market that store is located in. Each estimating equation includes controls for market type (medium markets, large markets, and metro markets) and separate indicator variables for each chain owner.[20]

$$(1) \log(\text{Weekly Grocery Revenue})_{ijk} = a + b\text{Opening}_{ijk} + c\text{Close}_{ijk} + \sum_{l} \delta_l \text{Market Type}_{ijk}^l$$
$$+ \sum_{j} \theta_j \text{Chain}_{ijk}^j + e_{ijk}$$

$$(2) \log(\frac{\text{Total Weekly Revenue}}{\text{Total Employees}})_{ijk} = a + b\text{Opening}_{ijk} + c\text{Close}_{ijk} + \sum_{l} \delta_l \text{MarketType}_{ijk}^l$$
$$+ \sum_{j} \theta_j \text{Chain}_{ijk}^j + e_{ijk}$$

$$(3) \log(\text{Grocery Square Feet})_{ijk} = a + b\text{Opening}_{ijk} + c\text{Close}_{ijk} + \sum_{l} \delta_l \text{MarketType}_{ijk}^l$$
$$+ \sum_{j} \theta_j \text{Chain}_{ijk}^j + e_{ijk}$$

For independent supermarkets it is not possible to control for the firm owner (since each firm owns a single store), so we estimate variants of equations (1)-(3) which do not include the chain indicators. Standard errors are calculated clustering at the market (k) level. For brevity we only report the coefficients corresponding to the opening and closing indicator variables in Table 5 (i.e. b and c in equations (1)-(3)).

Controlling for a store's chain and market type, we find the same general pattern seen in the unconditional means. Exiting stores tend to be the smallest and have the lowest revenue across retailer types, and newly opened stores are smaller and have lower revenue than continuously operated stores. The results for worker productivity (measured by total revenue per employee) are somewhat different. As before we find that exiting stores owned by chain supermarkets and supercenters are less productive than

---

[20] The omitted categories are continuing stores and rural stores.

both newly opened stores and continuously operated stores controlling for the chain owner and the market type. For chain supermarkets, however, newly opened stores are slightly more productive (roughly 1%) than continuously operating stores. More surprisingly, exiting independent supermarkets have virtually the same productivity as continuing supermarkets, while newly opened independent supermarkets are the most productive.[21]

Entry and Exit

There are many potential definitions of entry into a retail market. For instance, one of the primary factors differentiating competing retailers is the locations of the retailers' stores. When a retailer operating in a city opens up a store in a new neighborhood some consumers who had not previously considered the retailer as an option now consider the retailer as being in the choice set. In this sense, expansion within a broader geographic market could be viewed as market entry.

Operators of chain supermarkets often enter a region by purchasing an existing retailer and continuing to operate stores in that region under that retailer's brand name. Ahold, one of the largest U.S. operators of chain supermarkets in the U.S., does not operate any stores in the U.S. under its corporate name. Over time, Ahold has purchased supermarket chains such as Stop-and-Shop in the Northeastern U.S. and Giant Supermarkets in the Mid-Atlantic region, while maintaining their existing brand names. Although acquisitions of this type clearly represent a change in corporate control and the entry of a new firm (rather than a brand) into a region, the set of products available to consumers (brand names of retailers) do not change as the result of the transaction.

We study two types of entry which result in consumers being offered a new retail brand.[22] The first type of entry we define as "new firm entry" where a a firm with no presence in a market introduces a new brand to that market. The second type of entry is "banner entry" where an incumbent firm introduces an additional brand to that market. For example, during our sample period Delhaize began opening

---

[21] In their study of worker productivity of U.S. retailers Foster et al. (2006) found that continuously operated stores were the most productive followed by newly opened stores and that exiting stores were the least productive.

[22] Entry defined in this manner has been the topic of a number of recent retail studies focusing on entry by "big box" chains such as Walmart (e.g. Foster et al. (2006), Basker (2005), and Ciccarella et al. (2008)).

supermarkets operated as Bloom, a more upscale version of its traditional Food Lion supermarkets.[23] This type of entry is very different than new firm entry. While consumers are being introduced to a new product, the number of independent price setting firms has not increased. Banner entry is best viewed a form of new product introduction by incumbent firms, see e.g., Schmalensee (1978). Our definition of entry *does not* therefore include the sale of a local brand to a new firm that continues to operate retail outlets under the same trade name, such as the Ahold example discussed above. We also do not consider within market expansion – an existing retailer opening new stores of an existing banner in a market – to be entry.[24] We examine within market expansion and contraction in detail below.

We define exit as an event that causes consumers to lose access to a brand in a market. As with entry we consider two types of brand exit. We define "firm exit" as an event where both the firm and retail brand exit a market. We define a "banner exit" as an event where a retailer discontinues one of its retail brands but maintains its presence in the market as a big-box grocery retailer. Delhaize, for example, recently announced it will convert all but one of its Bloom stores in North and South Carolina to Food Lion stores.[25] Those markets that saw the conversion of Bloom stores to Food Lion as markets experienced banner exit. Parallel to entry, we do not view the sale of a retail brand to another corporate parent as brand exit if the subsequent owner continues to operate at least one store in an affected market under the original retail banner. Similarly, if a firm closes some but not all of the stores operating under a given banner we consider this to be within market contraction and not exit.

Panel A of Table 6 presents estimates of the overall rate of brand entry (defined as both firm entry and banner entry) including the mean number of entry events for each type of retailer and geographic market, the total number of entry events for each retailer type, and the total number of stores involved in entry between 2004-2009. We see that brand entry is relatively common among smaller firms. Roughly 63% of all entry events

---

[23] Supermarket News, March 14, 2011.
[24] As noted earlier, the geographic markets used in antitrust analysis are frequently more narrow than the geographic regions we have defined to be markets. As a result, what we define as a market expansion (e.g., a brand with operations in Los Angeles opening a store in Ventura) might be interpreted as market entry in an antitrust analysis (if Los Angeles and Ventura were separate antitrust markets).
[25] Supermarket News, 3/11/2011.

(1,605) are by independent supermarket firms.[26] The average medium sized city, for example, experiences 1.45 entries by new independent firms while metro markets experience, on average, 57 entries by independent supermarkets. Brand entry by small chain supermarkets is also common, with roughly 3.58 entry events in the average metro market, but less frequent than the entry of independents. Entry by large supermarket chains is much rarer. Large city and metro markets, on average, experienced only 0.83 and 0.68 entry events by large supermarket chains. Entry by supercenter and club retailers is also relatively unlikely in medium, large and metro markets. However, the reason entry is infrequent is because only a small number of firms operate these formats, and these firms were already operating in most large cities and metro areas by the beginning of 2004.[27] Finally, while entry of supercenters into rural/small city markets is relatively rare – the mean market experienced only 0.14 entry events – most supercenter entry occurred in these markets (223 of 247 entry events).

Panels B and C provide a breakdown of brand entry separately for firm entry and banner entry. By comparing Panels B and C, we see that small chain supermarkets, club stores, and supercenters are much more likely to begin operating a new brand in a market as a result of firm entry than by banner entry. For example, consumers in metro markets are about twice as likely, on average, to observe a new brand operated by a small supermarket chain entering a market (2.5) than to see an incumbent chain begin operating a new banner (1.08). In contrast, brand entry by large supermarket chains in metro and medium markets is, on average, about as likely the result of firm entry as incumbent firms introducing a new banner. For club and supercenter firms, most of banner entry is the result of WalMart opening Sam's club stores in markets where it is already operating supercenters or the reverse.

Table 7 presents the total number of brand exit events and the mean number of brand exit events by retailer and market type for all exits (Panel A), firm exits (Panel B), and banner exits (Panel C). As with entry, brand exit from a market is most common for independent and small chain supermarkets (rows 1 & 2 of Panel A). Brands operated by

---

[26] Recall that by independent firms operate a single retail outlet so that, by construction, for independent firms brand and firm entry are equivalent.

[27] Three retail brands (BJs, Costco, and Sam's Club) account for 99.3% of clubs stores and three brands (WalMart, Target, and Meijer) account for 93.2% of supercenters in 2008. At least one supercenter was operating in 11 of the 12 metro areas and in 39 of the 40 large cities at the beginning of the time period.

large chain supermarket retailers, however, are much more likely to exit than enter during our sample period. The mean metro market sees 1.75 brands operated by a large chain exit and only .83 brands enter. Further, brand exits by both large and small chain supermarkets involved many more stores than brand entries. The 219 entry events by large supermarket chains involved 473 stores while the 408 exit events involved 1117 stores. In contrast, exit by supercenter and club retailers were extremely rare. During our sample period we observed only 1 exit by a club retailer and 10 exits by supercenter retailers.

Panel B and Panel C of Table 7 disaggregate the statistics describing brand exit separately for firm exit and banner exit, respectively. There are two key findings from these breakdowns. First, market exit by small and large chain supermarkets is a much larger source of brand exit (1343 stores) than firms discontinuing one of multiple retail brands operated in a market (477 stores) during the sample period. Clearly, this is a period where small and large chain supermarkets are abandoning many of the markets they operate in. In contrast, brand entry by chain supermarkets is much more balanced between firm entry (460 stores) and banner entry (506 stores). Second, banner entry (Table 6 Panel C) and banner exit (Table 7 Panel C) appear similar for chain supermarkets; that is, firms seem to either add or subtract retail banners within the markets they operate with similar frequency.

Significance of Entry

Having measured the frequency of entry, it is natural to next measure the economic importance of entry. While an entrant could have many effects on a market (reducing prices, causing exit, increasing variety), we focus on measuring the size of an entrant brand after two years of market participation. Specifically, for each entering brand we calculate its revenue share by summing over all stores opened under that brand name in a market in the second year following the brand's entry.[28]

Figure 3 plots the 25th, 50th, and 75th percentiles of the distribution of the markets share of firm entrants calculated separately for each combination of retailer/market type.

---

[28]We have also estimated the size of entering brands in the first and third year following entry and find very similar results to those shown in Figures 3 and 4.

Figure 3 shows that all retailer types frequently attain significant revenue share in rural/small city markets in the two years following entry. For example, entering supermarkets owned by independents in the 25th, 50th, and 75th percentile of the market share distribution attain a market shares of roughly 4%, 7%, and 21%, respectively (top panel of Figure 3). Entering supermarkets owned by either small or large supermarket chains appear to gain larger market shares, with a median market share of roughly 14%. In rural markets, clubs and especially supercenters can attain very large market shares. The median supercenter in a rural/small city market attains an estimated revenue share of nearly 60%. Outside of rural markets, however, entrants rarely attain significant market shares in the two years following entry. In large city and metro markets we never observe the 75th percentile of the market share distribution rising above 7%. In medium markets we periodically observe supercenters become relatively large (the 75th percentile is roughly 16%). Hence, while we see that firm entry is relatively common, outside of the smallest markets, firm entrants rarely obtain significant revenue shares in the first years following entry.

New retail brands introduced by incumbent retailers attain revenue shares similar to *de novo* entrants in the two years following entry. This can be seen by comparing Figure 3 with Figure 4 which plots the 25th, 50th, and 75th percentiles of the market share distribution for incumbent firms chain engaged in banner entry. In rural/small city markets the median revenue shares for small and large chain supermarkets and club stores are very similar in Figures 3 and 4, roughly about 15% and 19% for small and large chain supermarkets and 18% for club stores. The revenue shares of "banner entrants" are even more similar to firm entrants in larger markets. In large and metro markets banner entrants very rarely attain market shares larger than 5%. The only significant difference in the market impact of firm and banner entrants is seen for supercenter entrants in rural/small city markets. While supercenter brands introduced by an incumbent retailer (most frequently WalMart) still attain substantial revenue share within the two years following entry (the median is larger than 30%), the distribution of revenue share for supercenter firm entrants is shifted significantly to the right of banner entrants (with a median revenue share of 60%). Again, we conclude that outside of the smallest markets, entrants rarely obtain substantial revenue shares.[29]

Changes in Store Composition within Markets

The entry and exit of a retail brand is not the only process that changes the set of retailing options available to consumers. Firms operating retail brands often expand or contract their operations within a market. This within market expansion and contraction by incumbent retail brands is responsible for more, often much more, of the change in the number of stores operated by brands within a market than either entry or exit. Our goal is here is to measure how much expanding brands grow and contracting brands shrink within the markets they operate during our sample period. To do this we first categorize each brand as either expanding (increasing the number of stores in operation), contracting (decreasing the number of stores in operation), or unchanged for each market and time period they are market participants. We then measure total expansion within a market in a time period as the number of stores added by expanding retail brands operating in that market in that time period. Similarly, aggregate contraction in a market is defined as the sum of all net reductions in the number of stores operated by contracting retail brands in a market in period t.

Table 8 presents the total number of stores added by expanding brands, and the mean number of stores added by expanding brands by retailer and market type. We see that market expansion is common and often results in significant growth by expanding brands within a market. The mean metro market, for example, saw expanding club retailers add 4.5 stores. In the average large city market expanding small and large chain supermarkets added 5.3 and 11.33 stores, respectively. To scale the relative importance of within market expansion reported in Table 8, we have calculated the number of stores added to markets as the result of both firm and banner entry in Table 9.[30] Comparing Tables 8 and 9, we see that in all but the smallest sized markets, within market expansion by incumbent retailers is much more important than entry in accounting for aggregate

---

[29] Our findings do not imply that entry does not have localized effects. Entrants almost certainly obtain a much larger revenue share within neighborhoods in which their establishments are located. Instead, our results show that outside of the smallest markets entrants rarely obtain significant revenue shares within two years in the relatively broad geographic markets we have defined.

[30] The store counts in Table 9 correspond to the entry events presented in Panel A of Table 6.

within market brand growth. For instance, in the average metro market growth resulting from entry of brands operated by large supermarket chains resulted in the addition of 10 stores while expansion by incumbent chains resulted in 24.25 new stores.

Similarly, within market contraction accounts for a large fraction of the reduction in the number of stores operated by brands within a market. However, as we show below the relative importance of contraction and exit is far more similar than expansion and entry in explaining brand growth. Table 10 presents the average number of stores closed by incumbent retailers in different sized markets during our sample period. As with exit, we see that within market contraction by club and supercenter retailers is quite rare (only 9 supercenters and 10 club outlets were closed by incumbent firms throughout the U.S.). Contraction by brands operated by small and large chain supermarket retailers were much more common. The average metro market saw 23.5 and 38.5 stores closed by contracting small and large chain supermarkets. To compare the relative importance of exit and contraction in explaining within market changes in the size of brands, we have calculated the average number of stores closed as the result of exit by retailer and market type during our sample period (Table 11).[31] In comparing Tables 10 and 11, we see that within market contraction is responsible for more store closures than exit by chain supermarkets in large city and metro markets. In the average large city market contracting brands operated by small and large chain retailers closed 4.3 and 10.3 stores while brands operated by exiting small and large chain supermarkets closed 2.28 and 8.1 stores. In medium sized markets, however, store closures caused by within market contraction are nearly the same as those caused by exit for chain supermarkets.

Within Market Changes in the Size of Retail Brands

We have shown that between 2004 – 2009 the number of retail outlets operated by big-box food retailers has remained roughly constant while relatively new retail formats, clubs and supercenters, have grown at the expense of traditional supermarkets. We have also shown that within market expansion and contraction by chain supermarkets explains a larger fraction of within market brand growth than either market entry or exit. In this

---

[31] The store counts in Table 11 correspond to the exit events presented in Panel A of Table 7.

section of the paper we construct two measures of market churn that describe how much the relative size of market participants changes within a geographic market between 2004 and 2009. The first measure focuses on changes that are most apparent to consumers: the change in the relative number of stores operated by retail brands (WalMart, A&P) that consumers observe in a geographic market. These changes are the result of both the expansion or contraction of incumbent brands and the entry and exit of new brands. The second measures the change in corporate ownership of outlets within a market which includes the entry of firms operating within a market as well as the sale of retail brands to different corporate parents. During our sample period a number of major food retailers, including Ahold and Albertsons, spun off large local brands to new firms. While these changes represented large changes in corporate control, they likely were transparent to consumers who observed the same brands operating in their local market.

We first measure churn in the number of stores operated by different brands within geographic markets during our sample period (2004-2009). We define churn as the amount of local market share (measured by retail locations) that changed hands among market participants (including entering or exiting brands). We begin by calculating each brand's (i) net growth in market j (brand growth$_{ij}$) as the difference in the number of stores it operated in 2009 and 2004 (where brand$_{ij2009}$ is the number of stores operated by brand i in market j in 2009):

$$brand\ growth_{ij} = brand_{ij2009} - brand_{ij2004}.$$

Within market j, we group brands into those that were shrinking (brand growth$_{ij}$ <0) and growing (brand growth$_{ij}$ >0) and then calculate the total number of stores that were added by growing brands or eliminated by brands that were shrinking. Because we are interested in measuring changes in the relative size of brands independent of changes in overall market size, we measure within market changes in relative size as the *minimum* of the proportional change in the number of stores either operated by growing or shrinking brands; that is,

$$\min\left(\frac{\sum_i (brand\ growth_{ij} \mid brand\ growth_{ij} > 0)}{\sum_i brand_{ij2004}}, \frac{\sum_i (brand\ growth_{ij} \mid brand\ growth_{ij} < 0)}{\sum_i brand_{ij2004}} \right).$$

For example, if within a market growing brands add 30 stores while shrinking brands close 20 stores, we would measure the net churn among brands as 20 stores (growing brands replaced 20 of the stores closed by shrinking brands). If big-box grocery retailers operated 100 stores in that market in 2004, we would say that market churn for that market is 20%.

We present the results from this calculation in a frequency histogram (Figure 5) separately for metro, large, and medium markets.[32] Figure 5 shows that churn in relative market position of retail brands is substantial in medium, large, and metro markets. Half of metro markets, for example, experience churn of at least 11% between 2004 and 2009; that is, in these markets growing brands increase the number of stores they operate by at least 11% while shrinking brands contract their operations by at least the same amount. In medium sized cities churn is somewhat smaller, the median market experiences churn of about 8% and 25% of markets experience no churn.

We conduct a similar calculation to measure changes in the corporate ownership of retail outlets. We calculate each firm's (i's) net growth (across all brands operated by the firm) in market j (firm growth$_{ij}$) as the difference in the number of stores it operated in 2009 and 2004 (where firm$_{ijx}$ is the number of stores operated by firm i in market j in year x):

$$firm\ growth_{ij} = firm_{ij2009} - firm_{ij2004}.$$

Within a market, j, we group firms into those that were shrinking (firm growth$_{ij}$ <0) and growing (firm growth$_{ij}$ >0) and then calculate the total number of stores that were added by growing firms or eliminated by firms that were shrinking. We then measure within market changes in relative size as the *minimum* of the proportional change in the number of stores either operated by growing or shrinking firms; that is,

$$\min\left(\frac{\sum_i (firm\ growth_{ij} \mid firm\ growth_{ij} > 0)}{\sum_i firm_{ij2004}}, \frac{\sum_i (firm\ growth_{ij} \mid firm\ growth_{ij} < 0)}{\sum_i firm_{ij2004}} \right).$$

---

[32] We have not presented results for small/city retail markets these markets tend to have very few total stores in operation (see Table 1). Changes in market configuration in these markets are rare and are typically the result of entry or exit.

We present the results from this calculation as a frequency histogram (Figure 6) separately for metro, large, and medium markets. There is considerably more churn among the size of firms operating within markets than retail brands within markets. When measuring churn among retail brands no metro market experiences turnover of greater than 25% (see Figure 5). In contrast, when measuring churn at the firm level one metro market experienced churn of 50%. The median market experienced firm turnover of about 12%, 17%, and 19% in medium, large, and metro markets, respectively. This is compared to the retail brand churn of 8%, 12%, and 11%, for the median market in medium, large, and metro markets.

V. Conclusion

This paper measures market dynamics within the big-box grocery retailing industry in the U.S. during a recent six year period. Despite being a mature industry -- with roughly 31,000 outlets each year during our sample period-- we observe substantial changes in the stock of stores in operation. In particular, the fraction of retail outlets operated as supercenters and club stores has grown rapidly at the expense of traditional supermarkets. However, even traditional supermarket retailers continue to upgrade the stock of stores they operated as supermarkets. During our sample period supermarket retailers opened new outlets representing roughly 2% of the stores in operation each year.

Our findings have important implications for studies of market dynamics. While entry and exit by small firms was a common feature of big-box grocery retailing, collectively entry and exit were responsible for only a fraction of the change in the relative size of retail brands operated within a market. Further when entry occurs, outside of the smallest markets, entrants rarely quickly gain a substantial share of market revenue. However, the failure of entrants to rapidly expand does not imply that local retail markets are best viewed as static oligopolies. In fact, we see significant turnover in the number of stores operated by different retail brands in most medium and large city and metro markets during our sample period. For example, the median metro market saw growing brands collectively expand their operations by 11% at the expense of shrinking brands. Our findings suggest that competition in these markets is significant and largely driven by interactions between firms operating incumbent brands.

Finally, we find that the retailers operating relatively new and differentiated products, clubs and supercenters retailers, are experiencing the greatest rate of growth (both as entrants and as incumbent retailers). This finding is consistent with Klepper and Thompson (2006) who predict that in mature markets entry (and presumably expansion) does not occur in existing submarkets (in our case traditional supermarkets) but rather in new submarkets (club stores and supercenters).

References

Baker, Jonathan. 2003. "Responding to Developments in Economics and the Courts: Entry in the Merger Guidelines," *Antitrust Law Journal,* 71, 189-206

Basker, Emek. 2005a. "Job Creation or Destruction? Labor Market Effects of Wal-Mart Expansion," *Review of Economics and Statistics,* 87 (1), 174-83

Basker, Emek. 2005b. "Selling a cheaper mousetrap: Wal-Mart's effect on retail prices," *Journal of Urban Economics,* 58 (2), 203-29

Basker, Emek and Michael Noel. 2009. "The Evolving Food Chain: Competitive Effects of Wal-Mart's Entry into the Supermarket Industry," *Journal of Economics and Management Strategy,* 18 (4), 977-1009

Basker, Emek, Shawn Klimek, and Pham Hoang Van. 2010. "Supersize it: The Growth of Retail Chains and the Rise of the "Big-Box" Retail Format," *mimeo*

Berger, Allen, Seth Bonime, Lawrence Goldberg, and Lawrence White. 2004. "The Dynamics of Market Entry: the Effects of Mergers and Acquisitions on entry in the Banking Industry," *Journal of Business,* 77 (4) 797-834

Ciccarella, Stephen, David Neumark, Junfu Zhang. 2008. "The Effects of Wal-Mart on Local Labor Markets," *Journal of Urban Economics,* 63 (2), 405-30

Courtemanche, Charles and Art Carden. 2011. "Competing Costco and Sam's Club: Warehouse Club Entry and Grocery Prices." NBER Working Paper 17220

Ellickson, Paul. 2007. "Does Sutton Apply to Supermarkets," *RAND Journal of Economics,* 38 (1), 43-59

Ellickson, Paul and Paul Grieco. 2011. "Density versus Differentiation: The Impact of Wal-Mart on The Grocery Industry" *mimeo*

Federal Trade Commission (FTC). 2008. *Horizontal Merger Investigation Data Fiscal Years 1996-2007.* Washington, DC: FTC

FTC. 2010. "FTC Challenges A&P's Proposed Acquisition of Pathmark Supermarkets," available at: http://www.ftc.gov/opa/2007/11/pathwork.shtm.

Geroski, P.A. 1995. "What do We Know About Entry*?" International Journal of Industrial Organizatio*n, 13, 421-440

Foster, Lucia, John Haltiwanger, and C.J. Krizan. 2006. "Market Selection, Reallocation, and the Restructuring in the U.S. Retail Trade Sector in the 1990s," *Review of Economics and Statistics,* 88 (4), 748-58

Goolsbee, Austan and Chad Syverson. 2008. "How do Incumbents Respond to the Threat of Entry? Evidence from the Major Airlines," *Quarterly Journal of Economics,* 123 (4) 1611-33

Haltiwanger, John, Ron Jarmin, C.J. Krizan. 2010. "Mom-and-Pop meet Big-Box: Complements or Substitutes?" *Journal of Urban Economics*, 67 (1) 116-34

Hausman, Jerry and Ephraim Liebtag. 2007. "Consumer Benefits from Increased Competition in Shopping Outlets: Measuring the Effect of Wal-Mart," *Journal of Applied Econometrics,* 22 (7), 1157-77

Igami, Mitsuru. 2011. "Does Big Drive Out Small? Entry, Exit, and Differentiation in the Supermarket Industry," *Review of Industrial Organization*, 38 (1), 1-21

Klepper, Steven and Peter Thompson. 2006. "Submarkets and the Evolution of Market Structure," *RAND Journal of Economics*, 37 (4), 861-886

Kosova, Renata and Francine Lafontaine. 2010. "Survival and Growth in Retail and Service Industries: Evidence from Franchised Chains," *Journal of Industrial Economics,* 58 (3), 542-78

Matsa, David. 2009. "Competition and Product Quality in the Supermarket Industry," *mimeo*

Syverson, Chad. 2008. "Markets: Ready Mix Concrete," *Journal of Economic Perspectives* 22 (1) 217-33

United States v. Baker Hughes Inc. 908 F.2d 981, 987 (D.C. Cir. 1990).

United States v. Syufy Enterprises, 903 F.2d 659,664 (9th Cir. 1990)

U.S. Department of Justice (DOJ) and FTC. 2010. *Horizontal Merger Guidelines.* Washington, DC: DOJ and FTC

Werden, Gregory and Luke Froeb. 1998. "The Entry-Inducing Effects of Horizontal Mergers: An Exploratory Analysis," *Journal of Industrial Economics*, 46 (4), 525-43

Tables and Figures

Table 1: Distribution of Store Size and Revenue of Conventional Supermarkets, Supercenters, and Club Stores

Retailer Type	Weekly Revenue ($ Thousands)							Store Size (Thousands of Square Feet Grocery Selling Space)						
			Percentile							Percentile				
	Mean	Standard Deviation	10	25	50	75	90	Mean	Standard Deviation	10	25	50	75	90
Conventional Supermarkets:														
Independent Store	102	67	50	70	90	125	175	13.5	8.7	5	8	12	17	25
Small Chain (2-100 Stores)	196	159	70	90	150	225	375	24.4	13.3	10	15	22	32	42
Large Chain (> 100 Stores)	289	136	150	200	275	350	475	32.3	9.4	21	26	32	38	44
Big Box Formats:														
Supercenter	926	339	475	675	925	1,175	1,350	61.9	10.7	49	54	65	69	72
Club Store	1,086	463	625	775	975	1,300	1,675	66.0	14.3	46	52	70	78	81

Source: Author calculations using grocery retail data provided by AC Nielson's Trade Dimensions database covering 2004 – October 2009.

Table 2: Mean Number of Stores and Grocery Revenue Share by Market Type and Retailer Type
Mean Stores and Revenue Share Within a Market Type

Retailer Type	Rural/Small City		Medium City		Large City		Metro	
	Stores	Share	Stores	Share	Stores	Share	Stores	Share
Independent	1.20	28.5%	6.88	7.2%	32.96	5.9%	191.28	7.6%
Small Chain (2-100 Stores)	1.04	26.0%	7.54	13.2%	29.30	11.3%	156.50	13.8%
Large Chain (> 100 Stores)	0.88	20.8%	12.94	32.1%	99.35	41.8%	370.67	46.7%
Supercenter	0.42	24.3%	3.72	36.5%	20.02	27.7%	32.81	15.1%
Club	0.02	0.4%	1.19	11.0%	8.75	13.3%	36.33	16.7%
Number of Markets in 2004	1,593		261		40		12	
Share of U.S. Population	12.7%		25.0%		26.6%		35.7%	

Source: Author calculations using grocery retail data provided by AC Nielson's Trade Dimensions database covering 2004 – October 2009.

Table 3: Total Number of Stores by Year and Retailer Type
Year

Retailer Type	2004	2005	2006	2007	2008	2009
Independent Store	7,623	7,511	7,386	7,149	7,113	7,119
Small Chain (2-100 Stores)	6,626	6,581	6,491	6,802	6,815	6,688
Large Chain (> 100 Stores)	13,901	13,488	13,090	12,883	12,875	12,937
Supercenter	2,174	2,463	2,760	3,040	3,256	3,329
Club	1,032	1,065	1,117	1,152	1,184	1,201
Total Number of Stores	31,356	31,108	30,844	31,026	31,243	31,274

Source: Author calculations using grocery retail data provided by AC Nielson's Trade Dimensions database covering 2004 – October 2009.

Table 4: Comparison of Means of Store Characteristics of Opening, Closing, and Continuing Stores

Store Characteristic		Independent Supermarkets	Chain Supermarkets	Supercenters	Clubs*
Weekly Grocery Revenue ($Thousands)	Continuing Stores	107 (72)	259 (143)	943 (318)	1,099 (451)
	Opening Stores	100 (52)	255 (150)	869 (342)	969 (373)
	Closing Stores	94 (49)	183 (103)	473 (288)	920 (256)
Log of Grocery Square Footage (Thousands)	Continuing Stores	14.2 (8.5)	29.9 (11.1)	61.6 (10.4)	66.2 (14.1)
	Opening Stores	11.4 (8.2)	29.8 (12.9)	61.0 (11.4)	64.7 (14.8)
	Closing Stores	13.0 (8.7)	28.7 (11.3)	53.4 (12.7)	64.8 (12.7)
Log of a Store's Total Weekly Revenue per Employee ($Thousands)	Continuing Stores	4.25 (2.62)	5.28 (3.12)	5.49 (2.53)	
	Opening Stores	4.35 (1.92)	5.19 (1.54)	4.76 (2.56)	
	Closing Stores	4.29 (2.67)	4.11 (1.63)	2.58 (2.16)	

Standard Deviations in parentheses.

* The number of employees in club stores was not included in the data, so that we could not calculate revenue per employee.

Source: Author calculations using grocery retail data provided by AC Nielson's Trade Dimensions database covering 2004 – October 2009.

Table 5: Regression of Store Characteristics on Indicators for Opening and Closing Stores

Store Characteristic	VARIABLES	Independent Supermarkets	Chain Supermarkets	Supercenters	Clubs*
Log of Weekly Grocery Revenue	Opening Stores	-0.0551***	-0.0507***	-0.154***	-0.128***
		(0.0183)	(0.0117)	(0.0140)	(0.0189)
	Closing Stores	-0.106***	-0.262***	-0.319***	-0.149***
		(0.0140)	(0.0123)	(0.0432)	(0.0302)
	Chain Fixed Effects	n/a	Yes	Yes	Yes
	Region Type Controls	Yes	Yes	Yes	Yes
	Observations	9778	25560	3405	1259
	R-squared	0.062	0.641	0.479	0.646
Log of Grocery Square Footage	Opening Stores	-0.280***	-0.0198*	-0.0443***	0.0158
		(0.0299)	(0.0116)	(0.00709)	(0.0180)
	Closing Stores	-0.164***	-0.0527***	-0.0684**	-0.0652***
		(0.0207)	(0.00914)	(0.0346)	(0.0231)
	Chain Fixed Effects	n/a	Yes	Yes	Yes
	Region Type Controls	Yes	Yes	Yes	Yes
	Observations	9778	25560	3405	1259
	R-squared	0.036	0.558	0.259	0.455
Log of a Store's Total Weekly Revenue per Employee	Opening Stores	0.0577	0.0144*	-0.110***	
		(0.0368)	(0.00857)	(0.0142)	
	Closing Stores	0.00426	-0.222***	-0.268**	
		(0.0171)	(0.0123)	(0.107)	
	Chain Fixed Effects	n/a	Yes	Yes	
	Region Type Controls	Yes	Yes	Yes	
	Observations	9778	25560	3405	
	R-squared	0.007	0.347	0.391	

Standard errors calculated assuming clustering by geographic market.

* The number of employees in club stores was not included in the data, so that we could not calculate revenue per employee.

Source: Author calculations using grocery retail data provided by AC Nielson's Trade Dimensions database covering 2004 – October 2009.

Table 6: Number of Entry Events, Stores Opened as a Result of Entry, and Average Number of Entry Events by Market and Retailer Type

Firm Type	Total US		Average Number of Events Within a Market Type			
	Entry Events	Stores Involved in Entry	Rural/ Small City	Medium City	Large City	Metro
Panel A: All Banner Entries (Brand Entry)						
Independent	1,605	1,605	0.15	1.45	7.70	57.00
Small Chain	383	492	0.10	0.51	1.08	3.58
Large Chain	219	473	0.07	0.25	0.68	0.83
Supercenter	274	289	0.14	0.15	0.13	0.25
Club	48	50	0.01	0.10	0.15	0.08
Total Count	2,529	2,909				
Panel B: Banner Entry through Firm Entry (Firm Entry)						
Independent	1,605	1,605	0.15	1.45	7.70	57.00
Small Chain	245	288	0.06	0.33	0.73	2.50
Large Chain	102	172	0.04	0.11	0.20	0.42
Supercenter	247	256	0.14	0.09	0.05	0.08
Club	28	30	0.00	0.06	0.15	0.08
Total Count	2,227	2,351				
Panel C: Incumbent Firm Introduces New Banner (Banner Entry)						
Small Chain	138	204	0.04	0.18	0.35	1.08
Large Chain	117	301	0.04	0.14	0.48	0.42
Supercenter	27	33	0.00	0.06	0.08	0.17
Club	20	20	0.01	0.05	0.00	0.00
Total Count	302	558				
Number of Markets in 2004			1,593	261	40	12

Source: Author calculations using grocery retail data provided by AC Nielson's Trade Dimensions database covering 2004 – October 2009.

Table 7: Number of Exit Events, Stores Closed as a Result of Exit, and Average Number of Exit Events by Market and Retailer Type

Firm Type	Total US		Average Number of Events Within a Market Type			
	Exit Events	Stores Involved in Exit	Rural/ Small City	Medium City	Large City	Metro
Panel A: All Banner Exits (Brand Exit)						
Independent	1,980	1,980	0.27	1.84	10.23	54.92
Small Chain	547	703	0.19	0.59	1.38	3.25
Large Chain	408	1,117	0.14	0.49	0.95	1.75
Supercenter	10	11	0.00	0.01	0.13	0.08
Club	1	1	0.00	0.00	0.03	0.00
Total Count	2,946	3,812				
Panel B: Banner Exit through Firm Exit (Firm Exit)						
Independent	1,980	1,980	0.27	1.84	10.23	54.92
Small Chain	360	463	0.14	0.37	0.63	1.58
Large Chain	292	880	0.11	0.36	0.53	0.75
Supercenter	10	11	0.00	0.01	0.13	0.08
Club	1	1	0.00	0.00	0.03	0.00
Total Count	2,643	3,335				
Panel C: Continuing Firm Exits Banner (Banner Exit)						
Small Chain	187	240	0.05	0.23	0.75	1.67
Large Chain	116	237	0.03	0.13	0.43	1.00
Supercenter	0	0	0.00	0.00	0.00	0.00
Club	0	0	0.00	0.00	0.00	0.00
Total Count	303	477				
Number of Markets in 2004			1,593	261	40	12

Source: Author calculations using grocery retail data provided by AC Nielson's Trade Dimensions database covering 2004 – October 2009.

Table 8: Total and Mean Number of Stores Added as a Result of
Within Market Expansion of Incumbent Brands by Retailer and Market Type

Retailer Type	Mean Number of Stores Added in Market Type				Total Stores Added
	Rural/ Small City	Medium City	Large City	Metro	Net Growth in Expansion
Small Chain (2-100 Stores)	0.04	0.88	5.30	26.75	822
Large Chain (> 100 Stores)	0.02	1.07	11.33	24.25	1,060
Supercenter	0.01	1.20	8.73	17.17	888
Club	0.00	0.08	1.40	4.50	130
Number of Markets in 2004	1,593	261	40	12	2,900

Source: Author calculations using grocery retail data provided by AC Nielson's Trade Dimensions database covering 2004 – October 2009.

Table 9: Total and Mean Number of Stores Added as a Result of Banner Entry by Retailer and Market Type

Retailer Type	Mean Number of Stores Added in Market Type				Total Stores Added
	Rural/ Small City	Medium City	Large City	Metro	Entry Events
Small Chain (2-100 Stores)	0.11	0.67	1.38	6.58	492
Large Chain (> 100 Stores)	0.09	0.52	1.93	10.00	473
Supercenter	0.14	0.18	0.18	0.42	289
Club	0.01	0.10	0.20	0.08	50
Number of Markets in 2004	1,593	261	40	12	1,304

Source: Author calculations using grocery retail data provided by AC Nielson's Trade Dimensions database covering 2004 – October 2009.

Table 10: Total Number of Stores Closed as a Result of
Within Market Contraction of Incumbent Brands by Retailer and Market Type

Retailer Type	Mean Number of Stores Closed in Market Type				Total Stores Closed
	Rural/ Small City	Medium City	Large City	Metro	Net Shrinkage in Contraction
Small Chain (2-100 Stores)	0.06	0.96	4.30	23.50	795
Large Chain (> 100 Stores)	0.03	1.17	10.30	38.50	1,227
Supercenter	0.00	0.00	0.18	0.08	9
Club	0.00	0.00	0.10	0.42	10
Number of Markets in 2004	1,593	261	40	12	2,041

Source: Author calculations using grocery retail data provided by AC Nielson's Trade Dimensions database covering 2004 – October 2009.

Table 11: Total and Mean Number of Stores Closed as a Result of Banner Exit by Retailer and Market Type

Retailer Type	Mean Number of Stores Closed in Market Type				Total Stores Closed
	Rural/ Small City	Medium City	Large City	Metro	Exit Events
Small Chain (2-100 Stores)	0.20	0.89	2.28	5.50	703
Large Chain (> 100 Stores)	0.16	1.13	8.10	20.33	1,117
Supercenter	0.00	0.01	0.15	0.08	11
Club	0.00	0.00	0.03	0.00	1
Number of Markets in 2004	1,593	261	40	12	1,832

Source: Author calculations using grocery retail data provided by AC Nielson's Trade Dimensions database covering 2004 – October 2009.

Figures

Figure 1: Estimated Share of Grocery Revenue by Retailer Type

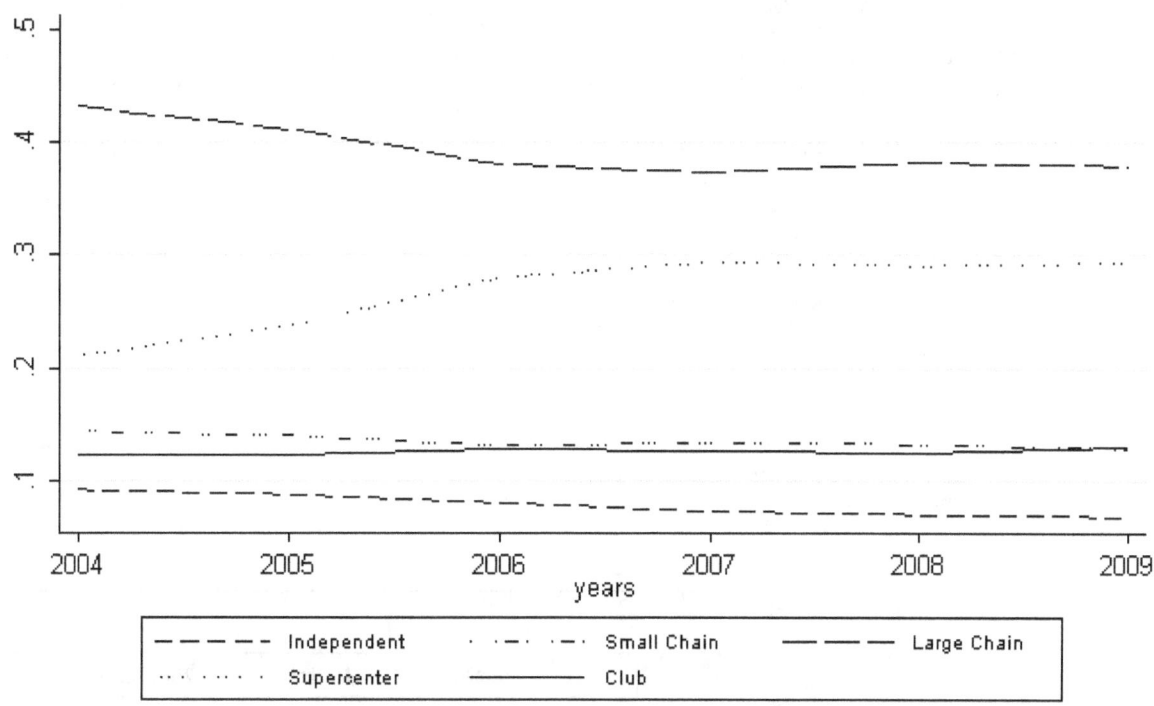

Figure 2: Ratio of Store Openings and Closings to Total Stores in Operation by Retailer Type

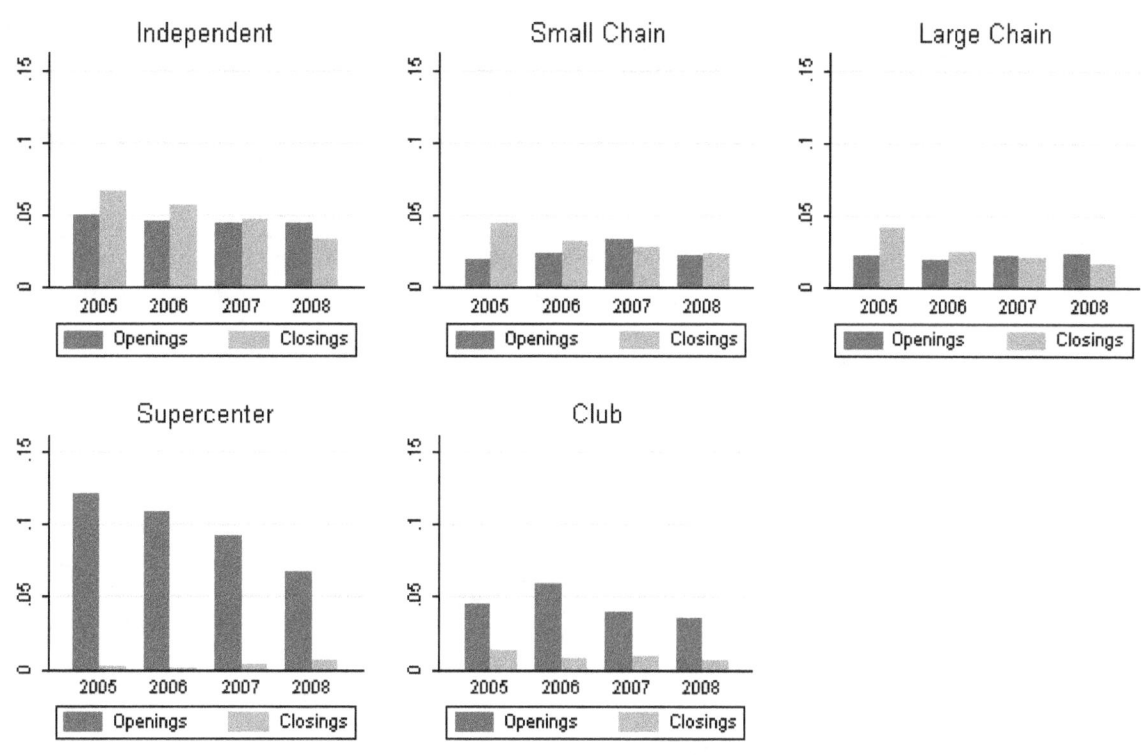

Figure 3: Distribution of Revenue Share of Entering Firms in Second Year Following Entry by Retailer and Market Type

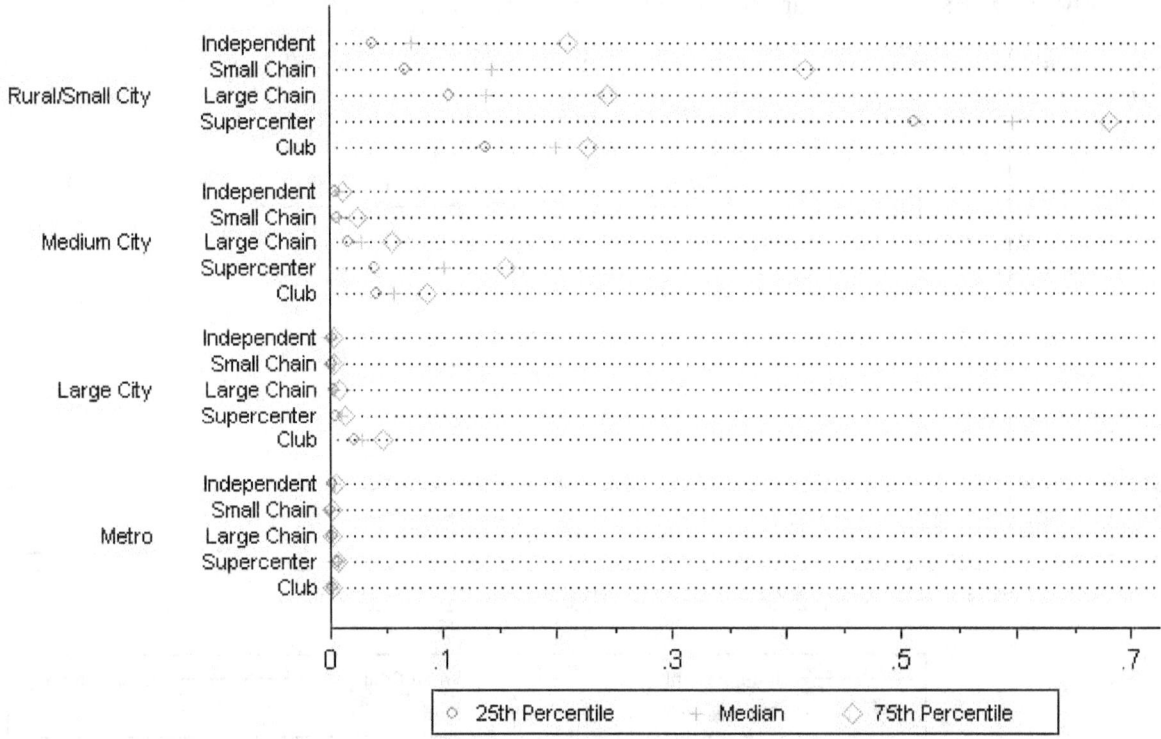

Figure 4: Distribution of Revenue Share of Entering Brands Operated by Incumbent Firms in Second Year Following Entry by Retailer and Market Type

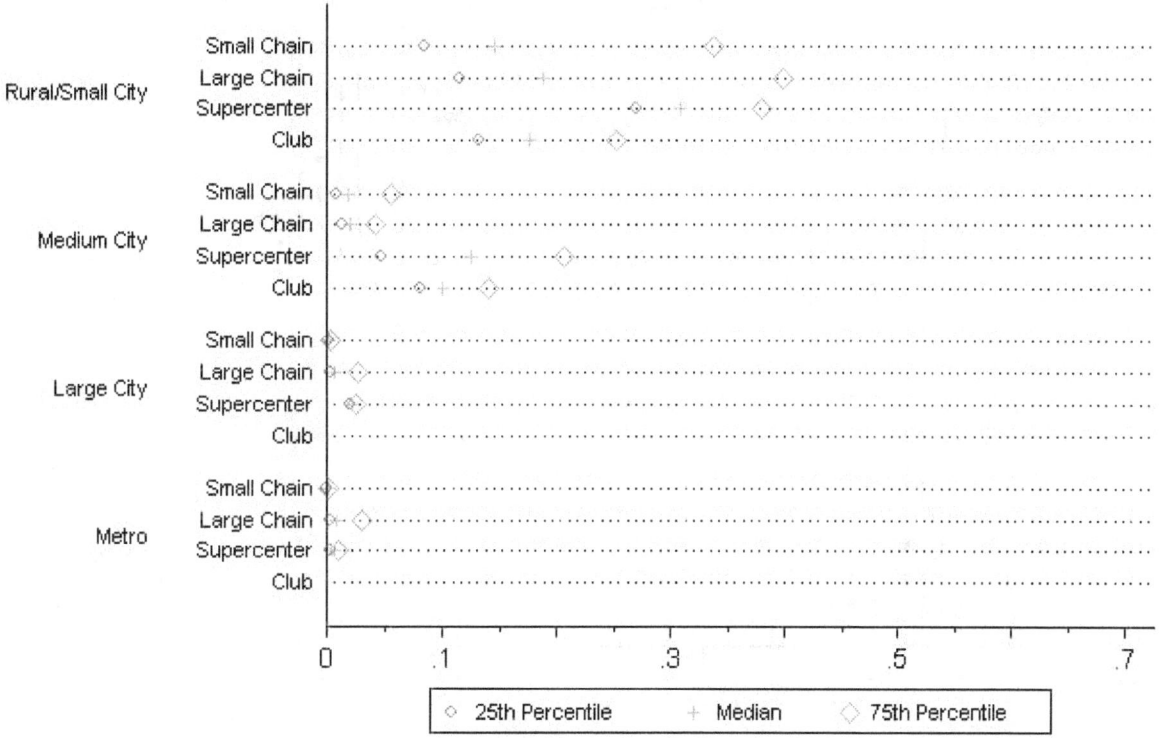

Figure 5: Frequency Histogram of Banner Churn by Market Type

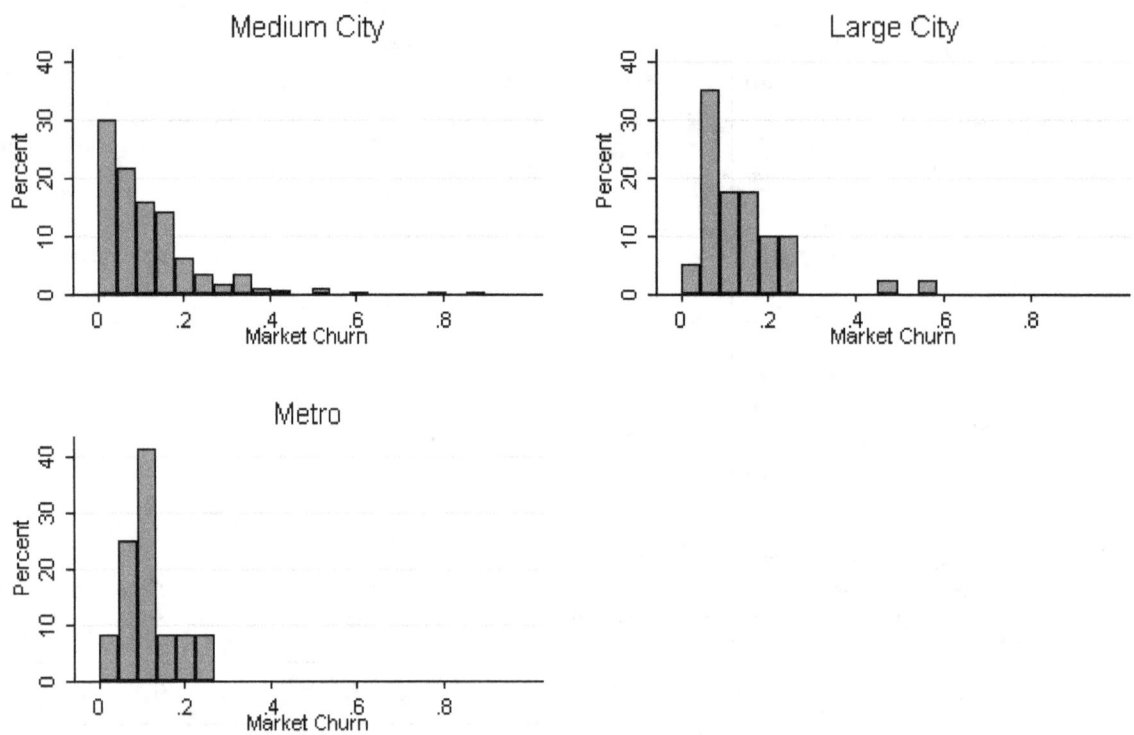

Figure 6: Frequency Histogram of Churn in Brand Ownership by Market Type

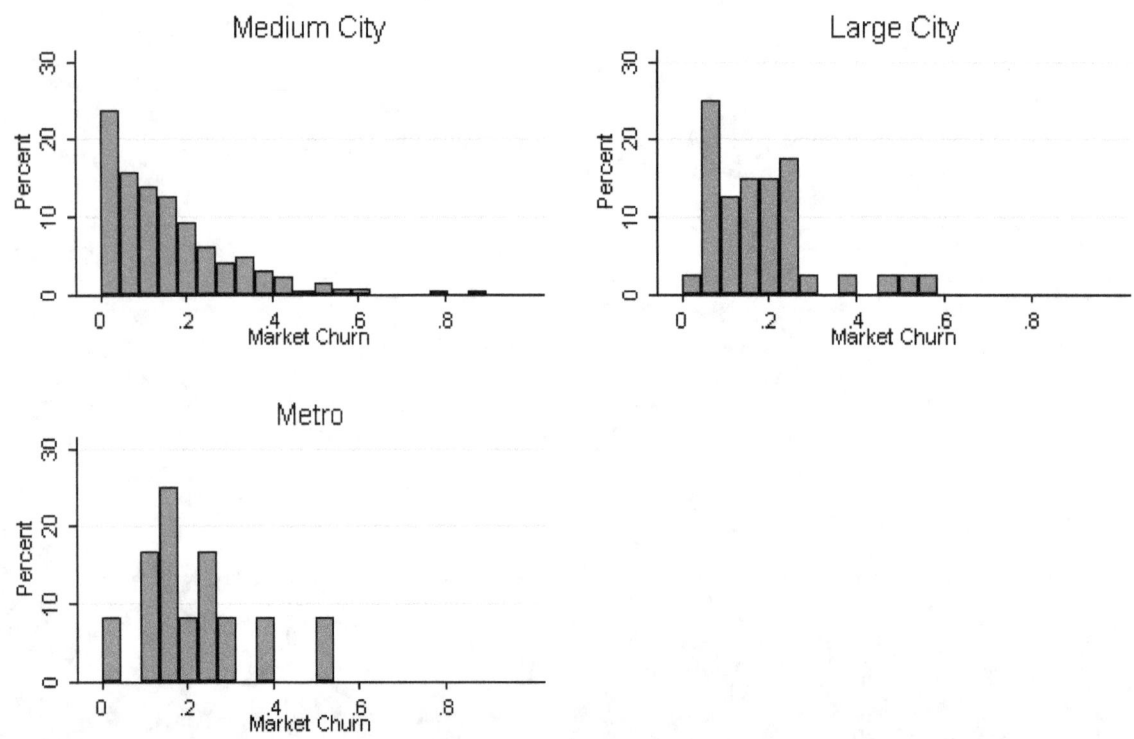